The

Blue

in the

Eye

of the

Girl

at

La Jolla

The Blue in the Eye of the Girl at La Jolla: New and Selected Poems
Copyright © 2020 by Eric Linder

978-0-931507-18-2

Published in the United States of America
First edition

Certain poems in this collection are works of fiction whose names, characters,
places, and incidents are products of the author's imagination. Any
resemblance to actual persons, living or dead, or to real entities or locales is
coincidental.

Loom Press, P.O. Box 1394, Lowell, MA 01853 and
15 Atlantic View, Amesbury, MA 01913
www.loompress.com
info@loompress.com

Author Photograph: Patty Brown Linder
Design: Dennis Ludvino
Printing: King Printing Co., Inc. Lowell, Mass.
Typefaces: Garamond Premier Pro and ITC Avant Garde Gothic Pro

for Patty, Hoshi, and Mika

I put out my hand and stroke
the fine, dry grit of their skins.
After all,
we are partners in this land,
co-signers of a covenant.
At my touch the wild
braid of creation
trembles.

— from "The Snakes of September" by Stanley Kunitz

Eric Linder

The
Blue
in the
Eye
of the
Girl
at
La Jolla

New and Selected Poems

Loom Press
Lowell & Amesbury
Massachusetts
2020

Contents

Sonofabitch Fork

Bright Passage   97

A Piece of Blue Sky   123

About the Author   129

Acknowledgements   130

Bamboo Bird Cage

Black & White Still · Outpost · Bamboo Bird Cage
Seven Carrots · The Cold War
How Far Is the Farthest Star? · Fishing Season
6/22 · Youngster Wading · Snow, a Boy's Dream
Pretzel Vendor · 7/11 · Suicide Season
Snadra Nad Our Snog · 8/2 · Lips
Priest Out of Nowhere · Nine-Foot Hoop · 8/31
In the Village · Dark Matter · For the Birds
Américain en Québec · 10/28
Now, Analyze This Poem

Black & White Still

Off the highway,
beyond plowed up snow,
gravestones, interrupted

dark daffodils
huddle in the act
of sucking in words.

Make a statement, you must.

Toss your black tongue
to the guileless
wing of the gull.

Outpost

Cape Breton Island

Gutted pig,
winter's meat
hung from crude tripod,
snout down,
inches from earth,
late October,
gray morning
of wind gusts,
father busy with guts
and rope, two children
and a black mongrel dog
in the way, woman
at window,
hair tied back,
spare, ruddy-cheeked,
fogs up one pane
watching mist
blow through.

Bamboo Bird Cage

She said the three-tiered
bamboo bird cage
in the window
of a Provincetown shop
was the perfect gift,
but he had reservations.
A bird's beak is strong.
It might break through.
They stood there awhile,
silent, trying to put themselves
in the bird's place.
The next evening
they returned and saw
a sign in the window:
Bamboo is Chinese steel
birds cannot destroy.

Seven Carrots

Clear a low table.

Place seven carrots there,
greens hanging

over the edge.

Unlatch the screen door.
Let it swing free.

Sweep debris
out of the way.

Give the place,
in general,
a tidy appearance.

Open the shades,
turn off the lights.

If moonlight enhances
your charade, dance.

Let loose garments flow.

If you want,
do a strip.

Who cares?

Then go to bed.

Sleep.

Any number
of rabbits

may come

calling.

The Cold War

Heidenreich had a way
with words. He never merely
pronounced. He enunciated.
You noticed this right off.
Good morning class. My name
is Mr. Heidenreich. The name
hung. Blood left his cheeks.
The hairless Neanderthal head
corroborated his declaration.
You studied the bite, counted
the gold fillings. You'd skipped
college and gone to dental school.

Heidenreich had favorite words,
culled undoubtedly from
years of punctilious study.
A *plethora* of events, never
a multitude, seldom a profusion.
Emily sat opposite me on the
semi-circle. We were both
front row. Heidenreich commanded
the open end, each class a
summit conference. Emily's
skirts were brown or gray
or navy blue, her blouses neat,
buttoned at the neck. She sat
straight, prim, her legs painfully
(for me) together, feet flat on
the floor, heel and toe touching,
penny loafers still in the shop window.

These were the Cold War
years. Eisenhower, Nixon,
Khrushchev. Heidenreich
championed Brinkmanship
and John Foster Dulles.
I studied Emily's legs. On
a beaver scale of one to ten,
she scored a definite zero.
Paula Bella Bella was a
different story. A giggly
girl, attractive even with
braces and too much makeup,
Paula was . . . well, precocious
is a nice word. One afternoon
on the bus home from school
Paula confided to me that
she had legs like peanut
butter. She demonstrated
what she called a smooth
spread to prove it.

Nights, disregarding the
ubiquitous bomb, I dreamed
of naughty Paulas and proper
Emilies trapped in bomb shelters
with me and the bare necessities.

How Far Is the Farthest Star?

He's at that age
when more
is better.

In time, he will come
to understand more fully
the limitations.

Who is the strongest,
fastest, smartest person
in the world?

At seven,
his possibilities
are endless.

As for me, he believes
I'm probably only about an inch
from being famous.

Fishing Season

The judge sprawls
on the bank
snorting legal perch.

The game warden
wades into the brook,
froggy hip boots,
badgering trout
with horseshoes.

Upstream,
a plump nude
unloads
beautiful barrels
of flesh.

6/22

Swedish ivy hanging,
hands frozen, green awe,
windows open, screens in,
cautious of summer.

Transistor radio static
adrift between stations.

Youngster Wading

Stick your finger
in your mouth, kid,
wade out, look back
at your hot, red mother
sprawling in shallow water,
getting her blue shorts wet.
You'll remember her,
heavy legs, blue shorts
soaked, twenty, thirty
years from now, when
thunder claps, and rain
comes down hard.

Snow, a Boy's Dream

Snow, a boy's dream.
His mother shouts upstairs.
He smells breakfast, looks
outside, no school.

He dresses warm, his
mother helps buckle the
boots, wrap the scarf,
open the door.

Out early to play, snow
knee-deep, sky dreary,
lingering flakes, mute
grey air. Cornstalks protrude
where the garden was.

Snow, a boy's dream,
vast untouched space.
Careful now, what path
to take. Sagging birches,
shortened oak, tulip, sassafras.
Dogwood by the stone wall, mock-blossomed.
Don't ruin it. Don't touch this space.

Now, his aunt who lives
next door, comes out smiling,
bundled warm. "C'mon," she says,
"let's build a snowman!"
The snow packs easily, the
ball larger and larger,
bigger than the boy.

Auntie lifts the head alone,
but that's not all. She
finds five stones to make
the mouth, two buttons for eyes,
and wait—
a carrot for the nose.
"My hands are cold," she says,
"I'll go in to make some hot cocoa.
You think of a name."

The boy falls down,
makes an angel.

Boys charge down the hill, shouting,
churning up snow. Butch, Doug,
even Johnny, who puked every day on
the bus the first week of school.
Butch, the bigger boy, assaults
the snowman. "C'mon," he says,
"the Confederates!" The boy remembers.
He is quick to help with the snow fort.

Confederates attack.

The frozen tassels
of his scarf
are numb fingers.

Pretzel Vendor

He lived downstairs
on the first floor.
He had some kind of deal

with the landlord.
He swept the stairwell
or something, shoveled snow,
brought the mail up, who knows?
He'd been a vandal,
shot streetlights out with a twelve-gauge.

So please *Reader's Digest*
print this story
of my most unforgettable character,

Jimmy, who went straight,
sort of, selling pretzels.

7/11

I unscrew both ends
of the telephone.
Silly things fall out.
Nothing resembles
our conversation.

Suicide Season

Groundhogs, Valentines
cast doubt. Shops
advertise roses,

candy, panties,
perfume, silk.
Night, the sky

is full of jewels.
Diamonds. Garnets.
Amethysts. Pearls.

Snadra Nad Our Snog

Snadra was parknig
her pnik Mustnag.
I was taknig off
my Foster Grnat snuglasses
waitnig for the snadmna.

Opnenig the livnig room
she said hello or somethnig.
I said nothnig nutil noticnig
the snu settnig behnid her
castnig her hair goldne strnads.

I begna snignig
day is dnoe.
I am glad you are not gnoe,
she said, it is no fnu
sleepnig here alnoe,

nad started nudressnig
nad taknig off my pnats.
I was gettnig a fnatastic
bnag out of the whole thnig
awaitnig the bnad nad our snog.

8/2

As you walk
toward the
stairs, I see
a moment of
space
through
your
flower
patterned dress,
through
the movement
of your thighs,
a moment
of obscure
light.

Lips

I was going nowhere.
She was going there, too.
She wore a last rose
from a bouquet
someone had given her
near her heart.

Her lips were red, but not ruby.
Red, like bloodworms,

upper and lower
quivering on hooks
when she spoke.

Priest Out of Nowhere

I was driving past
Saint Mary's Holy Redeemer,
cruising at a pretty good clip,
when this priest out of nowhere
crossed the street
right in front of me.
I didn't have to slam on the brakes,
but I had to slow down enough
to make me think
it's probably a lot worse luck
to hit a priest
than to have a black cat
cross your path.

Nine-Foot Hoop

I put up a basketball hoop
at the end of the driveway.
My friends come over and laugh.
They say, hey man, that ain't
regulation, it's only nine feet.
I'm almost thirty, not that tall.
I'll never make the NBA. All I
want to do is have some fun,
maybe stuff one once in a while.

8/31

Windowsills,
catchalls for
dead bees, saints, and
ripening tomatoes

In the Village

I am feeling down and
out, so I walk into a
bar, had to piss anyway.
The pissoir is grungy.

When I come out the
same couple is grappling
in the corner booth only
this time the guy's got

his tongue in her mouth.
I order a hard-boiled egg
and a beer. The bartender
is delighted to serve me.

Dark Matter

I woke up
at four
this morning
and not only
was my stomach
in distress
but I started
thinking about her.

For the Birds

We argued
night after night.

After that,
when we had decided

I should leave,
it was calm.

One morning,
her son said,

"It's very pleasant.
I can hear the birds."

Américain en Québec

"C'est la vie. C'est fromage."

"Non, monsieur. C'est dommage."

"Non, c'est fromage."

"Non, non! C'est dommage."

"C'est fromage."

"C'est dommage."

"Ce n'est pas dommage, monsieur. C'est fromage."

"Ah, monsieur. Oui. C'est fromage. Très bon!"

"Que será, será."

10/28

Starlings pock
October sky.
Black sparks
hit the fan
and jut off.

Though they jut,
jut, jut off
toward bleak
destination, they
are not lost.

One swoop
as quick light dims,
they gather
in dead oak,
fragment black iron

attracted to magnet,
each twitching
ornament
precisely placed.
Cold wind
howls through.

Nightfall, no apology,
no accident, no shape
dark ghost, too huge
to fly off.

Now, Analyze This Poem

At the library we hold our meeting
in a room with an open window at the end.
The fluorescent lights are harsh.
How do we endure this hardship?
Any one of us could get up and jump out.
Colorful, engaging, difficult, foolish.
Shall we vote? Draw straws?
Clockwise? Counterclockwise?
Fully dressed? Naked?
Hey, I've got an idea!
Let's each draw funny pictures
on the body with marking pens
of different colors. Now, analyze
this poem. Analyze each particle
as it drifts toward the open window.
Analyze the silence that follows.
Listen to the disquieting voice, the open window.

Sonofabitch Fork

Where I Live · Disappearing Phone Booth

Cow Dream · How Buildings Got Noses

Rebecca · Counter Intelligence · Bra · Fairy Tale

Dog Story · Pipe Dream · Cat

Leaf Mold: The 12-Step Program · Tuba Story

Sonofabitch Fork · Green Dragon With Pink Teeth

The Conversation · The Bathtub of Desire

Muzzle Opera Insanities of War Continue

Night Maneuver

The Man Who Had a Hundred Heads

Where I Live

It's a third-floor walk-up
in an old house on a cliff
above the river.
At night
I can see the skyline
of the city
and hear a mournful tug horn.
I can imitate that sound
by blowing over a beer bottle.
Sometimes I do it on the phone,
holding the beer bottle
away from the receiver.
Then I say,
did you hear that?
No one doubts it.
My landlady's Italian.
She opens my mail,
says she can't read
English too good.
She subscribes to
Business Week.
Her son drops by.
He's got a little
office furniture place
on a side street in town.
He says business is bad.
Next he's going bankrupt.
Then he shows up driving
a new black Cadillac.
Pay might be lousy,
but the benefits are good.

Disappearing Phone Booth

Crossing the bridge,
wind raw at my face,
I stop to lean over the railing.
I don't feel sick
or nothing, just pensive.
Fong dropped me a card,
said call from a phone booth.
I haven't heard from Fong for months.
I thought she was dead.
Now this card,
and it ain't even my birthday.
The day is foggy.
Here and there
colors ooze through.
A smear of mustard
as a taxi turns a corner.
A fire hydrant bleeds through
like blood.
Traffic lights blink out
dull, short warnings.
When I get to the phone booth,
it isn't there.
I'm standing on the corner
looking around in the fog
wondering where the hell it is.
That damned Madame Fong.
Then I think,
maybe I'm on the wrong corner.
So I walk up another block
and confirm my suspicion.
That damned Madame Fong.

Cow Dream

Clover heads
suck amethyst
from deep ocean sky
and decomposing
cow dung.

The large old cow
that has fallen
asleep
in the pasture
becomes cream
of mushroom soup.

Newly licensed kids
come to a screeching halt
in a polished
turquoise & white
'57 Ford convertible,
screaming
how unfucking unreal.

In a saucepan place one cow of soup.
Add one cow of water.
Use milk if creamier texture is desired.

How Buildings Got Noses

Once there was an architect
whose blue eyes matched the sky
no matter what the weather was.

Down in the swamps his companions
called him Swamp Thing,
but the name didn't stick.

Then one cloudy day, shut up
in a penthouse with a girl
he kept on a leash
and treated like a dog,

he got up and looked down
at buildings that didn't have noses
and decided each one should have one.

Rebecca

My name is Trigger,
and I don't know
if you know it or not
but I am going steady
with Becky. And I'll tell you,
if you don't stop writing Becky,
I'll be after your young ass.
And if you don't believe it,
just try me. This is not
a threat, it's a promise.
I read the letter she got from you
and I know all about you and her
at the races. I'm just sorry
I wasn't there to kick your ass,
you punk. And I mean it.
If she tells me of ever
getting a letter or a call
or anything from you again,
I'll be in New Jersey soon.
And I hope you just try me,
because I need a vacation.
I'll tell you what punk,
I have an uncle that told me
once some boy tried the same shit
with his girl and two days later
they pulled a .22 caliber slug
out of his head. So I hope
you look me up because
my uncle's gun is loaded
and I know how to use it.

Counter Intelligence

I did exactly
what the
African violet
told me to do.

Bra

The last few nights
walking home
from work,
I've passed a bra
on the side of
the road.
I wonder how it got there.
Did it blow
out of a laundry basket
from a passing car?
Did some girl
standing up
in a convertible
speeding by
at night
unlatch
and toss it off?
All I know
is this.
It's a 34B,
beige,
and probably
still there,
scrunched up.

Fairy Tale

The Big Bad Wolf,
fresh off the trail
from Grandma's house,
licks his lips twice,
then staggers in
at *Bill's Bar-B-Que*
and Grill on the corner
of Main and Potomac.
Locals, of course, call it
the corner of Main and Ptomaine,
but affectionately, because they
just love Bill's bar-b-qued meat.

Tired now and hungry again,
The Big Bad Wolf, in line
at the take-out, stands
there stupidly until
he finally gets his turn.

"Name please?" the perky girl
behind the counter inquires.

"Wolf." The Bad One says gruffly.

"With an *e* or without?" she asks.

"Without." he grumbles.

"What can I get you?" she asks pertly.

"Well, sweetums," he responds, licking his lips,
"I'm just gonna take out some of your ribs."

Dog Story

She named the dog Dylan. After the poet.
Not the singer. She loved that dog.
He tolerated it, most of the time.

He called it Dilly. Sometimes Dildo.
One day when he was taking it for a walk,
a woman came up and said, "What a cute dog.

What is it, a Scotty?" Embarrassed because
the exact kind of terrier it was slipped
his mind, he said, "I don't know.

It's not my dog." He skulked away sheepishly.
The day he left it was raining.
After he walked the dog,

he shoved it into the mailbox,
rear end first. It just fit. He said,
"Nice knowin' ya." Shut the box. Secured it.

Pipe Dream

My younger brother reaches over like a joke,
slits my throat,
pipe inside so big
it's ridiculous.
Now I have
this big gaping hole
in my throat
and a horrendously large
broken pipe
that takes both hands
to put back together.
So I walk
into the upstairs bathroom
holding pipe pieces together.
Plumber, head stuck
under the sink,
says what's wrong?
I figure I've done
a good enough job,
check it in the mirror.
Looks good to me.
Why call a doctor,
ask questions?
I've got two younger sisters,
too. Why cause trouble?

Cat

Cat's out of the bag.
That's what we heard
at the lunch counter.

Of course, we don't know
what the cat is
in the first place.

Now, there must be
some valuable cat
roaming around.

Collect all the cats.
Have a line-up.
Are you the cat that got out?

Leaf Mold: The 12-Step Program

1. The air smells like dog.

2. I don't smell nothin'. I don't smell no dog.

3. You ain't got the nose I got Motherfuck! The air smells like dog.

4. Do the mashed potato.

5. I'm all for foul play.

6. I think I'm going to eat you.

7. Don't let the mashed potato do you.

8. The mashed potato do me?

9. Bring the camera in close.

10. Do me! Do me!

11. Do me with the camera!

12. I love it how you drive me to a different state of bling.

Tuba Story

This is how
some time
in the past

two flutes
found a tuba
in the grass.

The tuba
had dragged out
a man who could

hardly blow.
The man
was a rag

at the lip
of the tuba.

Flutes flew around
taking wind in
letting it out.

Two flutes, free
and ecstatic,
a bedraggled man,

and a tuba.

Sonofabitch Fork

It's a stakeout.
I'm washing dishes in this sleazy joint.
Some jerk-off politician's
supposed to come in
with a briefcase full of money
to make a payoff.
We're supposed to grab him.
It's hot work.
I'm sweating my balls off.
There's this cute waitress, too,
but I don't want to blow my cover.
I'm washing dishes
and this one fucking fork
won't come clean,
all little bits of gunk
stuck on its prongs,
so I take out some steel wool
but this one sonofabitch fork
still won't come clean.

Green Dragon With Pink Teeth

One night
under a full moon
a dragon slept
as it had for ages.

The dragon
had slept so long
that houses
and condominiums

appeared on
its haunches
like barnacles
on the whale

that ate Jonah.
Weird birds flew
across the moon

screeching like banshees.
Up rose the dragon.

The Conversation

I'm sorry, Monica.
No, this is not Elvis.
No, honey, it's not.
Elvis is dead.
I know, I know. I'm sorry too.
Honey, I know.
I loved him too.
But Monica, sweetheart.
No, I swear,
this is not Elvis.
I know I sound like Elvis, honey.
Yes, I know you do.
I miss him too.
But Monica sweetie,
let me explain.
This is not Elvis.
This is the President.
That's right Monica.
The President. That's right, hon.
The one in the White House.
Uh, huh. The one you pass
in the hall. That thong thing?
In my office? Yes, Monica.
Yes, sweetheart. That's me.

The Bathtub of Desire

Original can be good.
Good on the other
hand might not be original.

In the bathtub
of desire it is
never so simple

as hot and cold.

Good can be
a vegetable
even as it
shatters like
glass.

Some patterns
emerge as
clouds drift away.

So who's the whack-job
who wrote this?

Don't deny yourself,
little angel.

Muzzle Opera Insanities of War Continue

I figured if
I sat there long enough
I'd see some action.

It won't help.
The crocodile will kill you.
You'll step in quicksand.

It won't help.
Words lock into earth
like carrots.

Night Maneuver

We have lived here two years this June.
See that house across the street?
They have lived there longer.

It is 1:15 a.m. Open the front door.
I'm going to sprint across the street.
What are the odds I'll get hit by a car?

If I make it, I'll knock on their door.
You'll see a light come on.
The door will open a crack, the chain still on.

I'll say Hi. I'm your new neighbor.
Then I'll sprint back. If I make it,
that should take care of the two World Wars.

The Man Who Had a Hundred Heads

No matter where he was,
he always looked good.
He had an alligator
and three gazelles,
some geese, a mole,
a moose that took up
half the room,
several different
mouse heads
that fit easily
in drawers.
Some cats, too.
And some rats.
And a basement full
of stuffed gorillas.
Days they say he worked
for a large corporation
as a headhunter.
He kept the hippopotamus
and the elephant out back
in the barn—hawk, dove,
pigeon, chickadee, blue jay
hanging from the beams.
You name it, he had it
in the bird department.

Here

Aardvark Constellation · Accident · Aerial
Amethyst · Amulet · Bonne Chance · Changes
Construct · Crack of Dawn · Dairy · Duplicity
Evolution · Frank · Gardener's Tip
Great Expectations · Here · Hives · Inches
Intersection · Item #4 · Just Dessert · Lemon Lime
Listless · Little Peach · Love Song · Lucky Day
Mystic Seaport · Odysseus · Poem · Punk Rock
Purple Haze · Religious Experience
Savage Mat · Separation · Sparks · Tibetan Tale
Universe Works · Warm Water · Wild · Youth

Aardvark Constellation

•   •

•

Accident

After the accident
my hand bled
like a limousine.

Aerial

That's it, he said.
Take that
weird-fucking-looking thing
out of your head.

Amethyst

Inestimable
virgins clamor
at doors, lips
puckered, purple, blue.

Amulet

People who wear
little bags of shit
around their necks
make me nervous.

Bonne Chance

Tattooed man
meets hefty woman
wearing pizza slice.

Changes

A polliwog and a quahog clam
ran away to Amsterdam.
The polliwog became a frog.
The quahog clam kept her mouth shut.

Construct

What other
of obvious
construct
can you
defend
from this?

Crack of Dawn

She bends to pick up panties
twisted on the floor
like a Mobius Strip.

Dairy

The dairy
got scary
when the cows
got hairy.

Duplicity

You can't be more
than one place at once
unless you're
fucking Houdini.

Evolution

AMOEBA
PLACENTA
SHOWER CURTAIN

Frank

Frank is here
to see you
with snot
on his shirt.

Gardener's Tip

Keep
Rosemary
Moist.

Great Expectations

The way
I started out
had nothing
to do
with this.

Here

Hello Ellie.
Hello Dave.

Already,
you suspect
something more
is going on.

Hives

Remember last year
when I told you
I was so worried
about dating this guy
I broke out in hives?

Next week,
we're getting married.

Inches

I once stood
inches from
a man made
entirely of
shoestrings.

Intersection

Hey
fat
fuck
get
out
of
the
way.

Item #4

The rear right corner
of the building
is sinking
into the ground.

Just Dessert

If I had known
you weren't coming,
I would have
baked a cake.

Lemon Lime

Lemon, Lemon, Lemon.
Lime, Lime, Lime.

Penny, Penny, Penny.
Dime, Dime, Dime.

Listless

Little Peach

The guy who owns
the Little Peach
calls the high school kid
who works for him
an abortion
because
he didn't price
the mustard right.

Love Song

Let us go then, you and I,
When the evening is spread out against the sky
Like a patient etherized upon a table—

Damn!

Fucking Shit, man!

I didn't write this.

Lucky Day

I am writing
to you today
because
I picked
your name
from my nose.
There were
thousands
of other names
in there, too,
but yours
was the only
one that came out.

Mystic Seaport

I have a brother-in-law
who lives in California.

Everyplace he goes
he says he's
the governor of Utah.

He's a good-looking guy.
Where the fuck's Utah?

Odysseus

Far have I traveled,
and many years,
to awaken startled
in this empty house.

Poem

As a poet,
it's my job
to trifle with
such things.

Punk Rock

That's
how much
you know
what's
going on
man,
in neon.

Purple Haze

The other day
when I woke up
I farted the first
two notes
of Hendrix's
"Purple Haze."

That's no
big deal,
I thought.

Then, when
I asked my wife

if she recognized
the tune,

she said no,
hum it again.

Religious Experience

God
was everywhere
except
where I farted.

Savage Mat

When you fall asleep
on the savage mat,

you wander through
room after room.

Dreams crash against
walls. Surf goes

wavy and metal. Bright
fish buzz fluorescent.

Separation

Split coils
of electric wire
snap at the night.

Sparks

I think I'll go
across the street
to that pay phone
and see if I can't
give Sparks a buzz.

Tibetan Tale

The abdominal snowman
crawls under your blanket,
sleeps on your belly.

The abominable snowman,
alias Yeti, we don't know
much about him yet either.

Universe Works

Every three billion years
green devil glides in
on inflatable horse,
steals piece of cheese.

Warm Water

The last time
you took

a bath
after me,

before
I got out,

I peed.

Wild

The mailbox
fell
way into
the prickly
bushes.

Youth

It's great
to be young
with vast choices
to abhor.

Bright Passage

Great Blue Heron · Walking Out

Fireflies · Half-Moon

The Blue in the Eye of the Girl at La Jolla

My Father's Garden · Heirloom · Dandelion

Full Circle · The Squirrel Tree · Lifeline

What I'd Like to Do · Earthquake

Falling Out of Love · Week at a Glance

Unexpected Deer · Lilac · Life · Bright Passage

Dusk · Ten Words That End in Light

Great Blue Heron

Alert. Motionless. Part of the fabric.
Tries not to be the dominant motif.
Blends in to its surroundings.

When it moves from one place
to another, on land, or in shallow water,
it moves like an s trying to form itself.

Aloft. Motion first sensed
from some unperceived point,
becomes a huge spread of wings.

Then, almost before it's been seen,
as if to say, truly there are angels,
it disappears again, leaving
the landscape as it was before.

Walking Out

Walking out across
the low-tide flats,

traversing great shapes of land,
memory of waves on the surface,

suddenly I am old and young,
transparent as pink air,

standing in shallow water,
peering down through

dizzy prisms of sunlight
at a hermit crab

in a moonsnail shell
scuttling along the bottom.

Fireflies

Waiting for you now,
on this cold winter night
somehow reminds me
of fireflies,

and in the dark darkness
in front of the house
of my youth, catching them
on a warm summer night,
then letting them go.

When finally, with jangling keys,
you walk through the door,
and sensing my agitation

and relief, ask if I was worried,
you know my shrug and pitiful stance
are the only mask I can find.

By now, I think,
my parents, both dead now,
would be home,

and, I as a child
having willed them home
safely, would be playing,
outside, dodging headlights,

catching fireflies
on a warm night
where fireflies abound.

Half-Moon

Driving home,
slowed down
in tourist jam,
I hear a woman,
hoisting her son
from traffic's harm
to the curb, say,
half-moon tonight,
I expect,
to admonish him
for one more thing
he's done,
as if the moon
I look up at now
is really sheared
in half.

The Blue in the Eye of the Girl at La Jolla

If there is
rhythm
to leaving
and coming back,
it is here

in this landscape.
Who would return
in this month at
this hour

but a traveler,
weary, scheduled back
from a climate

where warmth is
a state of mind?
Snow from
a recent storm

melts into ugly
tortillas along the highway, and
the only thing

that resembles
a margarita
is a water tower
on a distant bluff.

My Father's Garden

I know now
why my father
loved his garden.

I know why
from the heat
of an argument
he escaped there.

Why also it was
his beautiful
and constant
companion,

and why he
didn't need to learn
a new language
to speak to it
because he already knew.

I know how
an hour there
made his day
seem endless,

as his days were,
and why now
he has returned
to the earth,
his lover.

Heirloom

How are all the suns
a many-pronged clock?

What beneath the damp
and rotting leaves
do these hands remember?

What beneath the mesh
of tangled branch?

What lies beneath the moss
and fern? What acrid truth?

What beneath the intermittent star?

Furtively, we dream
beneath a somber sky.

The gears of time
are sure and resolute.

The golden thread
unerring and distraught.

What is buried
will not be spoken.

The long-held lie.

The wordless truth.

Dandelion

In life today, much is
in control and much is not.

Draw a line anywhere,
you'll see what I mean.

The dandelion, though,
is my favorite insurgent.

It grows anywhere,
especially in lawns.

But it's just as happy
in a crevice of dirt

at the base of a brick building
in a parking lot

full of broken glass.
No matter what,

it's a beautiful sight—
flowers, yellow, brighter

than the sun, leaves
the color of sea serpents.

And when it goes to seed
it's so magnificent

you want to pick it up
and blow it away.

Full Circle

If my mother had been
Native American, her name
would not have been Pocahontas.
It would have been Fear-Of-Feathers.

The sight of a bird
did not scare her. Nor did
the mere sight of a feather.
As long as *it* kept *its* distance.

But the possibility or act
of touching a feather or having one
touch her would send her into a frenzy.

I don't know if you noticed
or not, that big hawk
yesterday, out on Brevard, circling the funeral home.
That was Shirley. At first,
I don't think she knew what was going on. Then, circling
closer, noticing us all,
her family and friends, tearful, walking in and out,

I think she knew. I'm not sure
if she even made a sound.
Or tried to. But I know
it was her. Watching us.
Watching over us still. As always.

The Squirrel Tree

"And the angel of the Lord appeared to him in a flame of fire out of the midst of a bush; and he looked, and lo the bush was burning, yet it was not consumed."

— Exodus 3:2

Most of the leaves
from the oak
in my neighbor's yard
have fallen into mine.

I can rake them up
or leave them.

Today, I watch the squirrels.

In a moment there are twenty,
thirty, electric on the branches
of the oak. Amid this frenzy,

amid the flying fur of acrobats,
when one squirrel pauses, pulsing,
breathing, it clutches something

that resembles a heart.

Lifeline

From picking up
the burning log
to make the fire
brighter, my hands

smell like smoke.
I do not know
if I have had
past lives.

What concerns me
now, is this life.

Have I been
a hobo, saint
or king? How
should I know?

It's not like I'm
an architect
decorating walls

with shadows
and sinking feelings.

One of my earliest
memories from this

life was a lesson on
fire. When I was

a child of
three or four,

my father, burning
brush in the front
yard of our house,
warned me severely.

I grabbed the metal
bucket from the fire
anyway, burning my hand.

To look at it now,
I wouldn't say
it scarred me.

What I'd Like to Do

I'd like to sit
by a lake,
swat flies
for a month,
pretend
to fish,
become
a rainbow
trout, splash
up in a flash
of brilliant sun,
go down deep,
weep, come up
again, shine.

Earthquake

Many times, I held her
like a trembling bird.

In fact, once
my brother called
to ask where I was
during an earthquake

and I wondered
if there had actually
been one.

Falling Out of Love

To explain what happened
would be to describe
in a way that made sense
the guts of the clock
spilled on the floor.

How we got there
that night was not
by limousine.

It was, for each of us,
a long and spiraled path,
that here, at this point,
had become an entanglement—
the antithesis of love nest.

I remember it now,
not any better or worse
than if it happened yesterday—
for all of its qualities
are dismembered.

What we said
could not escape.
Words bounced off the walls.
Tapes replayed at furious speed.

There was burning heat
as the stuff of our lives
flew about the room.

It was as if simultaneously
the TV and sofa had exploded.

Yet, none of this is real.
The room went silent.
Nothing had been touched.

All night the nightbird shrieked.

Week at a Glance

MONDAY

We're not doing it
anymore.

She wants me to
buy the cow.

TUESDAY

Cold and blustery.

WEDNESDAY

Drove to Boston.

THURSDAY

Fucked like bunnies.

FRIDAY

SATURDAY

Moan from the bushes
above the surf.

Unexpected Deer

I am driving
at dusk,
when deer
cross the road.
The car in front
slows down, stops
where the road
veers off
up over a ridge.
The deer, a doe
and her fawn,
pause like cut-outs
in an aura
of fading sun,
then, on the other side,
crash through brush.

Lilac

So that though
light is dim,

this is not
a dull room,

one lilac,
lavender.

Life

There is no one left
who speaks my language.

That's what you hear
old people say.

Until you realize
one day, that by degree,

this is what you are becoming.

I don't imagine old age anymore.
Its old beard awaits me.

When the autumn moon shines down
on my young wife's face,

I listen to the sounds of night.

Bright Passage

Autumn,
early morning,
scent of wood smoke,
brightly polished hearse,
windows rolled up,
driver's face barely visible,
approaches and continues steadily uphill,
past the first white house,
and the second white house,
black gleam on the curve, gone.

Dusk

I should know by
now that that
blue blue silk
fits like a glove.

Ten Words That End in Light

Sunlight, moonlight, candlelight,
taillight, nightlight, daylight,
plight, blight, flight, delight.

A Piece of Blue Sky

A Piece of Blue Sky

You are in bed but you are not asleep. It is dark in your room. The light from a streetlamp projects the window over your bed onto the wall at the foot of your bed. The shape of the projected window is distorted due to the angle of light. If it bothers you, you should pull down the shade, but it doesn't bother you. Instead, you want to get up and look through the window at the foot of your bed. This is silly because you know you can't see anything through this window, but just the same, you'd like to try. You have never tried it. You cannot be one hundred percent sure.

You are still looking at the window, not through it. On the other side of the window is a closet where you keep your clothes. The window, if placed in its proper perspective, would have you standing off to one side. About fifteen feet off to one side, you think. That reminds you of standing about fifteen feet off to one side of a barn window on an incline so you are looking up.

It is a large window, a magnificent window, with a warm friendly personality, and it is the only window on the side of the barn. It is morning and it is summer. The sun is behind you warming your neck and the backs of your arms. It makes you warm now to think of it. You can smell the grass and the freshly turned soil. There is a small yellow butterfly and a sunflower much taller than you. The barn is dark inside so the window is reflecting what is outside, which, from where you are standing, is blue sky. It is a deep blue sky, and seeing it reflected in the window makes it even darker. The barn is red. Faded red. A red that has blended with its surroundings through many seasons. The paint, especially the paint on the window frame, is brittle and cracked and peeling off. When you turn your head fast to look for the butterfly, the barn blurs into the sky to make purple. Where is this barn? You think about it. You don't know.

You are still in bed. It is winter and it is very cold outside. So cold that there are ice ferns on the kitchen window downstairs. So cold you could gingerly remove the crystal halo from the streetlamp and wear it. This thought chills you. Not enough to make you stop looking at the window on the wall, but enough to keep you in bed under warm blankets. You raise your right hand to make a shadow puppet. You make a rabbit that doesn't look like a rabbit and a crocodile that doesn't look like a crocodile. Your rock doesn't even look like a rock. What if the windowpanes were black and when you raised your hand you made a white shadow; a white shadow as bright as the mantle in a gas lantern; so bright you couldn't look directly at it without hurting your eyes? The window is still there on the wall and the panes are pale white.

One morning on your way to work, a sunny day, walking down Ninth Avenue, an autumn day, crisp and just cool enough to wear a sweater, walking past the markets where men in soiled white aprons busily arranged crates and barrels of fresh produce, walking briskly down a crooked path of color, large bright apples, mute earthy beans, crates of new knotty wood with labels larger and brighter than labels on packages of firecrackers, you suddenly stopped. On the edge of the sidewalk leaning against a wall, there was a window, frame and all, much like the one over your bed now. The wood was painted gray and chipped. The four panes of glass were dirty but unbroken. You picked it up. It was a little heavier than something you wanted to carry, but you wanted it anyway. That morning on your way to work carrying a window, you passed a man leaning against a wall holding a metal cup containing a few coins. He was shaking the cup so you would hear the coins in the cup as you passed. The man had no eyes. Just flesh. Empty spoons. No glass eyes. No dark glasses. He was shaking his cup. You were carrying a window. Did you toss a coin into the cup? You think about it. You can't remember.

You carried the window into the building where you worked and stepped into an elevator already crowded with people. They all had eyes. Two each. You are sure of that. It's a short ride up in the elevator, and all those eyes looked at you at least once. It's a short ride up in the elevator. But you were carrying a window. Not a briefcase. A window.

At the eighth floor you got off the elevator and carried the window to the room where you worked. The room was one room in a complex of rooms, situated in the central portion of the building, surrounded by long, artificially lit corridors, flanked on the outside by offices that had windows, but not windows accessible to you. Of course, once in a while you could inadvertently walk into one of those offices to look out a window and say, "I'm sorry, I must be in the wrong office."

That morning, Diane, one of the young women you worked with, was already there. You were on time and so was she. Both of you knew there were no windows in the room except the one you were carrying. There were five desks in the room and each had a chair and a person to sit in the chair. Only one desk, however, was backed to a wall. It seemed like the logical choice. You placed the window on the desk, leaning it against the wall.

Later that morning, everyone was seated at their desks, and it appeared that everyone in the room was happy to have a window, even though it was only a window leaning against a wall. Except for Bernard. Bernard had no work to do. He sat at his desk. He sat there, chin resting on his clasped hands, staring at the window. He sat there for more than forty-five minutes, no work to do, staring at the window. Then he got up. He walked out of the room as if he was going out for coffee or a brief errand. Bernard did not, however, come back to his desk, and it was almost lunchtime before other people in the room wondered what happened to Bernard. No one in the room ever saw Bernard again.

You are still in bed staring at the window on your wall. Someone in your closet is trying on your clothes, deciding what to wear. You haven't gotten up to look through the window at the foot of your bed because you think you can't see through it. You are not aware that someone in your closet is buttoning the cuffs of your red plaid shirt. In less than five minutes this person will climb through the window you thought you couldn't see through.

The person will gently place a hand on your left foot. You will think, at first, that you should scream. But you won't, because it will feel good. It will be a warm hand.

Having placed the window on Bernard's desk, you stood back for a look. Then you adjusted it slightly to the right, so it was, in your eyes, perfectly centered. It was a good window even though it was not performing to its full capacity as a window. You turned to Diane and said, "Kiss me." You often said that, to her in particular. You'd said it to her so often, in fact, that it had become a private joke. Her desk was behind yours and you would turn to her at the most inappropriate moment and say, "Kiss me." She would look up and laugh.

Neither of you were sitting at your desks now. You were both standing in an uncluttered space of shiny floor behind Bernard's desk. When you turned to Diane and said, "Kiss me," she smiled graciously, gently placed her arms around your waist, and kissed you. It was a good kiss and you will never forget it. It wasn't the best kiss you ever had, but it was a good one, involving both sets of lips.

It makes you warm now to think of it. Like looking at a window of an old red barn on a summer day from fifteen feet off to one side on an incline looking up.

Acknowledgements

"Intersection," "Universe Works," "Evolution," "Accident," "Inches," "Dusk," "Ten Words That End In Light," "Frank," "Sparks," "Poem," "Aerial," and "Construct" appeared in issues of *The Quarterly*, edited by Gordon Lish, published by Random House.

"Bright Passage," and "Walking Out" were published in issues of *Harvard Magazine*, edited by Donald Hall.

"Cat" was published in *Light Year: The Annual of Light Verse and Funny Poems*.

"Dog Story" was published in *Mudfish*.

"Snadra Nad Our Snog," "7/11," and "Seven Carrots" were published in *The Bellingham Review*.

"Bamboo Bird Cage" was published in *The Cape Cod Compass*.

"Fishing Season" and "6/22" were published in issues of *Tightrope*.

"The Blue in the Eye of the Girl at La Jolla," and "10/28" appeared in *Merrimack: A Poetry Anthology*.

Thanks to Paul Marion for his editorial eye and companionship on our long journeys as fellow poets; to Denny Ludvino for his patience and design expertise; and to Tyler Keyes for his assistance in bridging the gap between the technical and the poetic. Special thanks also to Patty for walking beside me every step of the way.

ERIC LINDER received his BA from the University of Evansville in Evansville, Indiana. After working briefly in New York City in advertising, he moved to Chelmsford, Mass., where he owned The Chelmsford Bookstore for five years. He has owned and operated Yellow Umbrella Books in Chatham, Mass., on Cape Cod since 1980. He has performed his work in Boston; Lowell; and Andover, Mass; Chelan, Wash.; and on Cape Cod at various venues including Night of New Works at the Academy Playhouse in Orleans and the Cape Cod Cultural Center in Dennisport. He lives in Eastham where he recently discovered a meteorite in his back yard while digging turnips.